Be Still, and Know

Inspirational Poetry by
David Robinson

Stargate Publications

Be Still and Know
by David Robinson

British Library Cataloging - in - Publication Data.
A catalogue record for this book is available from the
British Library.

ISBN   0-9525689-0-x

Published by Stargate Publications

Printed by The Print Shop Of Cannock

"Be still, and know that I am God..."

Psalm 46:10

Dedicated to the Source that
inspires,
understands,
loves.....

Introduction

The following collection of poems are simplistic in nature, personal, and are in themselves complete meditations. It is my heartfelt wish that all who read these inspirations will feel a vibration that resonates at a deep level of their being.

There is an essence in each poem, conveyed in the space around the words and there is a personal message for all who read on.

So to capture that essence
be still and know...

Be still,
and know,

I am that which you seek
that all evading peace,
you will find Me in the stillness
once found, will never cease.
I am found in all things
if you would but try to begin
to be still, and full of awareness
and then you will take Me in.

Be still,
and know,

when you come as a child
with innocence and humility,
I will give you the help
to bring you stability;
I will give you the keys
to the door of your heart,
for once in that room
we will never part.

Be still,
and know,

that when you pray
I hear every word,
when you cry from the heart
it goes not unheard;
I will answer your call
when the time is right,
when your candle is ready
to yield more light.

Be still,
and know,

I am with you wherever you are,
you are like a wandering star;
I am your universe forever still,
you will find Me everywhere if you will.

Be still,
and know,

that in the halls of meditation
is a gallery of special art,
where all the pictures painted
are with colours from the heart;
some visions cannot be captured
because they are made of light,
but they are there awaiting
for those whose love is right.

Be still,
and know,

you are My reflection
of what I seem,
I am there beside you
when you dream,
when you climb a mountain
I am beside you still,
so reflect this in My glory
and in My loving will.

Be still,
and know,

that I am your friend
always by your side,
I am there to help you
and always be your guide.
Through the times of trials
and the seasons of your life,
I am there to give you strength
to take away your strife.
So share with me these moments
when you need a hand to hold,
with My heart to ever warm you
to keep you in My fold.

Be still,
and know,

that in searching for Me constantly
through the stillness of your mind,
in being patient for those moments
that you will surely find;
My outstretched hand to guide you,
My voice to calm your fears,
My love to always warm you,
to carry you through the years.

Be still,
and know,

when you are all alone
then call on Me by name.
Talk with Me -
the feeling is just the same;
share with Me your burdens
so that I may lend a hand,
to give you time for gathering
the strength to make a stand.

Be still,
and know,

that I am your refuge
in the corners of your mind,
in the moment of despair
there I will be your find;
through times of sorrow
with many things to cure,
I am your strength
with a love to endure.

Be still,
and know,

All your many problems
that surround you by the score,
are only meant to help you
and grow a little more.
By reason and understanding
and hearing what is said,
will only allow your love to glow
and keep you in good stead.

Be still,
and know,

that on your life's journey
there are many things to learn,
at each and every crossroad
you have to take a turn;
remember as you have to walk this path
of happiness, sorrow and fear,
you will always see an ending
because I am always near.

Be still,
and know,

when I call on you to share with Me
the full experience of your life's song,
it matters most of all your learnings
that you have learned from right and wrong;
so be not afraid of the shame you have
for I will forgive every sin,
if you would but let go of guilt
so your heart can take Me in.

Be still,
and know,

all the gifts from Me
that make Me part of you,
can only grow and blossom
if you can flower too;
it is in the sharing of these gifts
the ones you cannot see,
like the giving and the loving
that brings you close to Me.

Be still,
and know,

when My love stirs from deep within
it opens up a door,
allowing all your precious gifts
to burst forth from within your store.
Your gifts are like the flowers
allow their fruits to be,
pluck them, give them freely
for all humanity.

Be still,
and know,

that when they sound their trumpets
it is their talent that they bring,
their heartstrings have been plucked
so hear their music sing.
Let their efforts stir you
to wake you from your sleep,
so share your gifts with joy –
they are not yours to keep.

Be still,
and know,

that when on earth while you are living
in sharing My love in all that you do,
by giving and caring for every soul
will bring many gifts to you.
Faith, hope and truth are a few
of the building blocks you earn,
to take you forward with wisdom
and love, you took the trouble to learn.

Be still,
and know,

to harmonise with nature
will bring you close to Me,
to be part of all creation
will bring you humility;
appreciate the loving
that you give to mother earth,
in time she will return to you
the mirror of your worth.

Be still,
and know,

if you cannot look at nature
and hear the plaintive call,
then you will not feel the glory
and the love within it all;
you will be without a knowing
of the beauty at your hand,
to feel the love of nature
and the fruits of this her land.

Be still,
and know,

I am your creator
I live in many things,
my spark I leave behind
to see the light it brings;
minerals, plants and animals
have their purpose too,
every time you remove their light
it severs Me from you.

Be still,
and know,

in every plant that grows
in every bird that sings,
remember to treasure them
for I am in all things.
They are there to show you
to share without complaint,
giving themselves submissively
with the patience of a saint.

Be still,
and know,

that I am in your very breath -
the breathlessness of wonder
when you adore creation,
the breath of a loving kiss
that you give in adoration,
the breathlessness of pain
when your body is put to test,
the breath of departure
when you are laid to rest.

Be still,
and know,

When one has reached the passing
from your world to the next
be sure to remember
the words beneath the text;
"Your loved one goes before you
because their day is done,
they go to prepare the way
for another who has not run".

Be still,
and know,

That when one travels from your world
in permanence and alone,
be sure that I will meet them
and take them to their home.
I will find them there a place of rest
to sleep and gain strength anew,
then they will see horizons
that only they can view.

All the love that they have given
is stored within a chest,
which will then be opened
when they have had their rest.
This chest of jewels will open
and radiate such wealth,
of happiness and pure pleasure
which will restore their health.

Do not grieve in sadness
nor for your pity's sake,
send them onward with your love
for you will follow in their wake.
They may come and visit you
to cheer your lonely day,
so be sure you are not crying
it may well bar their way.

Be glad that they have found a place,
that they can call again
a place of solace like their home,
where they are free from pain.
Many mansions will they visit
to suit the seasons of their soul,
but they will do their choosing
to reach the greatest goal.

Know your loved one will come yet closer
for we shall never part,
their love will only magnify
in the bosom of My heart.

Be still,
and know,

your loved ones are a thought away
from the message of your heart -
a bond of common language
while you are apart.
Attract them not for pity's sake
to bring them very near,
they can only come no closer
than the barrier of your fear.
So after they are parted
and you have set them free,
share with them my happiness
in bringing them to Me.

Be still,
and know,

that your life is like the seasons,
with little growth to start,
but with an age that comes and goes
you will have something to impart.

Winter is your childhood
as your spirit sleeps,
but it awakens to the spring of youth
and all the love it reaps;
through the growth of middle age
all your flowers bloom,
into the fruits of autumn
to prepare you for your room.

This room is in My mansion
the result of your life's goal,
by the total of experiences
of the seasons of your soul.

Be still,
and know,

Know yourself and you will know the universe,
love yourself and you will love your friend,
love your friend and you will love your enemy.
Love one thing but desire it not
and you will love Me
for I am in all things,
for as you love you experience Me,
I am that feeling of love -
I am the object of your love.
I am both Giver and Receiver,
I am in you, you are part of Me.
Where that love is I am,
I am that love.
I am that I am.

Be still,
and know,

Allow Me to grow within you,
through your love.
You feel Me,
you will know me.
Take Me to your heart
and you will know the universe -
all that ever was,
all that ever is,
all that ever will be.
As you know all things,
then you will know Me also,
for I am in all things.
You are in Me and I am in you.
We are in each other.
We are one.